When I Die

What's Next?

A Message of Hope

By Harry Carter

Just as people are destined to die once, and after that to face judgment, so Christ was sacrificed once to take away the sins of many; and he will appear a second time, not to bear sin, but to bring salvation to those who are waiting for him.

— *Hebrews 9: 27-28*

*This work is dedicated
to the glory of God.*

About the author

Harry Carter is a Christian and lifelong educator who has served as a college provost, interim college president and professor. He has also served in the US Navy and the Air National Guard. An avid student of the Bible, the author is an active member of First Baptist Church in Charleston, SC. He has written two other books that share his beliefs about the Bible and what it means to be a Christian.

All Bible verses quoted are from the New International Version unless otherwise stated. A complete list of references and resources for further study can be found at the end of this pamphlet.

Published August 2017

Introduction

In a previous work, *My Understanding, Reflections on God, Life and Death,* I described four personal encounters I have had with the death of a loved one. These experiences included the deaths of my father, mother, wife of a close friend and my brother-in-law. No doubt you also have experienced the death of a family member, co-worker, friend or stranger. My experiences led me to reflect on the question What Happens When I Die?

Charles H. Spurgeon, a prolific writer and leader in the Reformed Baptist movement, wrote a devotional that speaks directly to this question. Born in Essex, England in 1834, Spurgeon was pastor of the New Park Street Chapel in London for 38 years. You can find a compendium of his daily devotionals on the web. One of his works is a daily devotional entitled *Morning and Evening.** From this collection I have selected his morning devotion for May 11 which cites the following text from Matthew 28.

> [20] and teaching them to obey everything I have commanded you. And surely I am with you always, to the very end of the age.

Spurgeon focuses on the phrase, "**I am with you always, to the very end of the age.**"

---

*Originally published in 1865 and republished many times, the full citations for Spurgeon's work and others cited in this booklet are in the reference section.

The following quote from the May 11 devotional offers an eloquent picture of what happens when we die.

> Death's black extinguisher must soon put out your candle. Oh, how sweet to have sunlight when the candle is gone! The dark flood must soon roll between you and all you have. Then wed your heart to Him who will never leave you. Trust yourself with Him who will go with you through the black and surging current of death's stream, and who will land you safely on the celestial shore and make you sit with Him in heavenly places forever.

John Piper also reflects on what happens after our death. The preaching pastor at Bethlehem Baptist Church in Minneapolis Minnesota for 33 years, Piper is a renowned theologian with an impressive body of work. He was born in Chattanooga, Tennessee and grew up in South Carolina. He graduated from Wheaton College, Fuller Theological Seminary (MDiv) and the University of Munich (Doctor of Theology). His sermons and teaching are available at *desiringgod.org*.

In 1993, Piper preached a series of four sermons on the topic of what happens when you die which I discovered as we were concluding this work. He offers four reasons why this topic is important to all of us.

1. **It matters infinitely what happens to you after you die.**

The Bible describes our life on earth as a vapor that we breathe on a cold morning. However, time after death is described as ages of ages. In other words an infinite amount of time . . . forever. So it does matter infinitely what happens after I die.

2. **Facing eternity has an amazing effect on sobering us out of religious delusions.**

This question forces us to think about whether our faith is real or if it is just an emotional cushion to help us face the bumps in life.

3. **Thinking about death and eternity helps keep God as the center of our lives by testing whether we are more in love with this world than we are in love with God himself.**

Do we count it as gain to die and be with God and Christ, or do we fear the loss of the things in this world?

4. **When the biblical truth of this theme grips you, it frees you from fear and gives you the courage to live the most radical, self-sacrificing life of love.**

Embracing this biblical truth gives us the daily courage to not lose heart as we go through the often painful and depressing decline in our health as it diminishes in old age. If we really believe in Heaven and life after death, then we can say with confidence "to die is gain."

John Piper's sermon series can be viewed at http://www.desiringgod.org/series/what-happens-when-you-die/messages.

We now have a glimpse of what a well-known Christian pastor has to say about this critical topic. So, let's begin examining this question – what happens when I die – for ourselves.

So, let's start examining the question – What Happens When I Die?

DEATH CAN COME AT ANY MOMENT

Let's begin with an incident that occurred more than five decades ago . . . the unexpected death of President John F. Kennedy. Newspaper reports tell us the president was riding in an open car in a motorcade during an official visit to Dallas, Texas on November 22, 1963.

According to *The Warren Commission Report*, the president was sitting in the right rear seat with Mrs. Kennedy seated to his left. Sitting directly in front of the president was Governor John B. Connolly of Texas and directly in front of Mrs. Kennedy sat Mrs. Connolly. The vehicle was moving at a slow rate of speed down an incline into an underpass that led to a freeway route to the Dallas Trade Mart where the president was to deliver an address.

Three shots were heard and the president fell forward, bleeding from the head. (Governor Connolly was seriously wounded by the same gunfire.) At that moment, Bob Jackson, the *Dallas Times Herald* photographer, turned to the direction where he heard the shots and saw a rifle barrel disappearing into an upper floor window of the nearby Texas School Book Depository Building. (*Washington Post, November 23, 1963*)

Shortly following the wounding of the two men, the car sped to Parkland Hospital in Dallas where Dr. Malcolm Perry was one of the physicians waiting. In a telephone conversation on November 23, 1963, Dr. Perry described the procedures that were performed in a futile effort to save the president's life.

President Kennedy sustained a massive wound of the head and a second much smaller wound to the lower neck. A tracheostomy (an incision in the windpipe made to alleviate an obstruction to breathing) was performed by extending the latter wound. At this point bloody air bubbled from the wound revealing an injury to the right lateral wall of the trachea. Doctors then made incisions to the chest and administered infusions of blood, saline solution and oxygen in a desperate effort to save the president's life.

Yet despite these measures, cardiac arrest occurred and closed chest cardiac massage failed to get the heart beating again. President Kennedy was pronounced dead approximately thirty to forty minutes after being shot. *(The preceding information comes from the Warren Commission Report Appendix IX entitled JFK Autopsy Report.)*

The remains of the president were flown to the National Naval Medical Center in Bethesda, Maryland for postmortem examination. In the following days, the nation watched the funeral and collectively grieved over the sudden death of the young president.

The death of President Kennedy was one the most memorable and nationally mourned deaths of my lifetime. If you do not remember this event, you have no doubt read about it in American history.

Despite the heroic efforts to save the life of one of the most powerful men on earth, the death of President Kennedy illustrates an inescapable truth. Death occurs in a number of different ways . . . but it always occurs.

At the time of this writing, I am almost 73 years old and have been married to Brenda for 49 years. There are a number of conclusions I could draw from those facts but one important one is this:

Most of my life is over!

So I realize that at some point (in the not too distant future) I am going to die. My death will probably not be as dramatic as President Kennedy's was . . . but dead is dead!

Therefore, I ask myself this question: **What happens when I die?**

Not many people want to think about their own death because it can be scary, confusing or unsettling. Have you thought about this question? Think of the people you know who consider death to be "off in the future" and so cannot bring themselves to write a will. Most people do one of three things when facing their own mortality. They either

- ignore it,
- fear it, or
- deal with it.

The purpose of this booklet is to look at this question and think about some answers . . . so let's deal with it!

The first verse of the Bible (Genesis 1:1) says, "**In the beginning God created the heavens and the earth.**" If I believe this statement. . . and I Do . . . then God made everything we know and everything beyond all we know. Based on that fundamental belief, I conclude the following.

1. God is Sovereign – that is He ordains everything. He knows it is going to happen and He makes or allows it to happen.

2. God Is Good – that is His purposes are good. His purposes may be clear to us or they may not be clear but they are ultimately for good. In Genesis 1:31, when He finished His creation, "God saw all that He had made, and it was ***very good.***"

3. God is Truth – that is He has given us the truth. In ancient days He spoke through the prophets, then through the apostles, now through His Son and the Holy Spirit. His word...the Bible...is The Truth.

Therefore, I approach our topic from a Christian perspective. However, you must answer the question – **what happens when I die** – based on your own beliefs.

If you are not a Christian, my hope and prayer is that God, through this process, will change your heart. If you are a Christian, my hope and prayer is that this discussion will strengthen your faith.

THE STARTING POINT

Dr. Martyn Lloyd-Jones (1899 – 1981) is one of many who have reflected on the issue of our own mortality. A Welsh Protestant minister, author and medical doctor, he was pastor of the Westminster Chapel in London for almost 30 years. The following two quotes from his book, *The Quiet Heart,* provide a great introduction to our journey.

> Do we in fact believe that the great goal that is confronting us is the goal of getting to the Father and getting to heaven?

> . . . you and I are passing through this world of time. We have to die in any case, and the one thing that matters is how we can arrive at God and Heaven and spend our eternity in the glory. That is what I am interested in, and that is the only thing that we should be interested in, because a day is coming when we will have no other interest and we shall be leaving the world and everything else behind. Then we shall be facing that unknown eternity and our great question, 'How can I know God?' should have already been resolved at that time.

Now, imagine yourself on a path and you come to a fork in the path. You have several choices of which direction to go. But to keep going, you must choose one. That's how we will approach this big question. We will go along a path and make several decisions regarding what we believe as we move forward.

THE FIRST DECISION

The first decision is **does one believe in a god or not**? Notice I am not specifying which god at this point. If one does not believe in a god, then the answer to our big question

("What happens when I die?") is as follows: nothing . . . it is over . . . there is no after-life.

If one does believe in some god, then that person is following some religion of the world. Almost all the world religions have a position on the after-life.

THE SECOND DECISION
The second decision is **what kind of after-life**? The religions of the world vary greatly on this question. But the two main choices are

- Heaven or Hell, and
- some form of reincarnation.

The Bible speaks of only Heaven or Hell. So I believe that we are all bound for one of those two final resting places. One of many significant passages on this topic is found in the book of Luke, Chapter 16.

> [19] There was a rich man who was dressed in purple and fine linen and lived in luxury every day. [20] At his gate was laid a beggar named Lazarus, covered with sores [21] and longing to eat what fell from the rich man's table. Even the dogs came and licked his sores.
>
> **[22] The time came when the beggar died and the angels carried him to Abraham's side (heaven). The rich man also died and was buried. [23] In Hades, where he was in torment, he looked up and saw Abraham far away, with Lazarus by his side. [24] So he called to him, "Father Abraham, have pity on me and send Lazarus to dip the tip of his finger in water and cool my tongue, because I am in agony in this fire."**
>
> [25] But Abraham replied, "Son, remember that in your lifetime you received your good things, while Lazarus

received bad things, but now he is comforted here and you are in agony. [26] And besides all this, between us and you a great chasm has been set in place, so that those who want to go from here to you cannot, nor can anyone cross over from there to us."

[27] He answered, "Then I beg you, father, send Lazarus to my family, [28] for I have five brothers. Let him warn them, so that they will not also come to this place of torment."

[29] Abraham replied, "They have Moses and the Prophets; let them listen to them."

[30] "No, father Abraham," he said, "but if someone from the dead goes to them, they will repent."

[31] He said to him, "If they do not listen to Moses and the Prophets, they will not be convinced even if someone rises from the dead."

The rich man and the beggar died. One went to Heaven and one went to Hell. The reason was not based on what they "had" while on earth. The reason had to do with their hearts. It is clear to me that we all arrive at one of these two destinations after we die. Please notice that this is our **final destination** . . . for eternity!

THE THIRD DECISION

This decision involves what I believe about the following question.

What determines whether I end up in Heaven or Hell?

For most religions of the world, Heaven or Hell (or one's status in the after-life) is based on earthly performance. That means that I must earn my way into Heaven based on doing "good." The other fork, Christianity, says that Heaven is a gift from God and I cannot work my way into Heaven.

Again, the Bible is clear on this question as we can see from Ephesians, Chapter 2. Please look at verses 8 and 9 very carefully.

> As for you, you were dead in your transgressions and sins, [2] in which you used to live when you followed the ways of this world and of the ruler of the kingdom of the air, the spirit who is now at work in those who are disobedient. [3] All of us also lived among them at one time, gratifying the cravings of our flesh and following its desires and thoughts. Like the rest, we were by nature deserving of wrath.
>
> [4] But because of his great love for us, God, who is rich in mercy, [5] made us alive with Christ even when we were dead in transgressions—it is by grace you have been saved. [6] And God raised us up with Christ and seated us with him in the heavenly realms in Christ Jesus, [7] in order that in the coming ages he might show the incomparable riches of his grace, expressed in his kindness to us in Christ Jesus.
>
> **[8] For it is by grace you have been saved, through faith—and this is not from yourselves, it is the gift of God— [9] not by works, so that no one can boast.** [10] For we are God's

handiwork, created in Christ Jesus to do good works, which God prepared in advance for us to do.

I hope you are still with me. Let's review where we are:

1. I acknowledge that I will die someday.
2. I believe that there is life after death.
3. I believe that life after death is either Heaven or Hell for eternity.
4. I believe that I cannot earn (work) my way into Heaven.

Let's look more closely at belief #4.

Why can't I work my way into Heaven? If that were possible, how good would I have to be? I have committed a lot of errors in my life. The Bible calls them sins. I have done those things that God says in the Bible that I should not do.

Think about the Ten Commandments. I have lied and I have coveted. I have not always honored my father and my mother. I have placed other gods ahead of God. For example, there have been times in my life when I chose family or career or golf or tennis over God. My point is that I know I have committed many sins over the course of my life. In fact, my record of sins is enormous.

Consider Matthew 5:48: **"You therefore must be perfect, as your heavenly Father is perfect".**

God is perfect (holy) and will not tolerate imperfection (sin). But none of us is perfect . . . especially me! So, how can I work my way into Heaven given all this sin in my life? I cannot possibility do enough to "pay back" for the wrongs I have done over the course of more than seven decades.

How about you? How do you judge your own life against God's commandments? The Bible says that the two greatest commandments are as follows (Matthew 22).

> [34] Hearing that Jesus had silenced the Sadducees, the Pharisees got together. [35] One of them, an expert in the law, tested him with this question: [36] "Teacher, which is the greatest commandment in the Law?"
>
> [37] Jesus replied: **"'Love the Lord your God with all your heart and with all your soul and with all your mind.' [38] This is the first and greatest commandment. [39] And the second is like it: 'Love your neighbor as yourself.'** [40] All the Law and the Prophets hang on these two commandments."

I don't know about you, but I know I have not kept those two commandments and they are given as the greatest of God's commandments. So, I conclude that I am in real trouble. I need some way of getting rid of all these sins I have accumulated or I will not be able to go to Heaven . . . I will end up in Hell.

Now at this point, we may be feeling either really bad or very guilty. We may feel that there is no hope for us. I have felt that way about my sins and my after-life.

BUT THERE IS GOOD NEWS! THE GOOD NEWS IS THE GOSPEL OF JESUS CHRIST!

God is completely just . . . He holds completely to His word. He does demand perfection. He does not "look the other way" and say that my sin is okay. Every sin must be punished. But, He is also merciful and has designed a way for our sins to be removed.

His plan is described in many places in the Bible. Perhaps the most famous is in the book of John Chapter 3.

> [16] For God so loved the world that he gave his one and only Son, that whoever believes in him shall not perish but have eternal life. [17] For God did not send his Son into the world to condemn the world, but to save the world through him. [18] Whoever believes in him is not condemned, but whoever does not believe stands condemned already because they have not believed in the name of God's one and only Son.
>
> [19] This is the verdict: Light has come into the world, but people loved darkness instead of light because their deeds were evil. [20] Everyone who does evil hates the light, and will not come into the light for fear that their deeds will be exposed. [21] But whoever lives by the truth comes into the light, so that it may be seen plainly that what they have done has been done in the sight of God.

Let's make a few very important observations about the passage we have just read.

1. God gave/sent His son . . . God took this action . . . not me
2. Whoever believes on Him shall have eternal life . . . so the offer is for everyone
3. If I believe, I am not condemned . . . Heaven is for me
4. If I do not believe, I am condemned **already** . . . because of my sins.

Because this is so critical, I want us to look at two other places in the Bible where sin and grace are covered. Let's look again at Ephesians Chapter 2.

As for you, you were dead in your transgressions and sins, [2] in which you used to live when you followed the ways of this world and of the ruler of the kingdom of the air, the spirit who is now at work in those who are disobedient.

[3] All of us also lived among them at one time, gratifying the cravings of our flesh and following its desires and thoughts. Like the rest, we were by nature deserving of wrath. **[4] But because of his great love for us, God, who is rich in mercy, [5] made us alive with Christ even when we were dead in transgressions—it is by grace you have been saved.**

Please notice verses 4 and 5. Because God loves us so much, in His great mercy, He changes us from being completely lost (dead) in our sins to being alive . . . found. He does this based on His grace and not on what we do or do not do.

Finally, let's look at the first chapter of Peter's first letter.

[3] Praise be to the God and Father of our Lord Jesus Christ! In his great mercy he has given us new birth into a living hope through the resurrection of Jesus Christ from the dead, [4] and into an inheritance that can never perish, spoil or fade. This inheritance is kept in heaven for you, [5] who through faith are shielded by God's power until the coming of the salvation that is ready to be revealed in the last time.

[6] In all this you greatly rejoice, though now for a little while you may have had to suffer grief in all kinds of trials. [7] These have come so that the proven genuineness of your faith—of greater worth than gold, which perishes even though refined by fire—may result in praise, glory and honor when Jesus Christ is revealed.

^{8} Though you have not seen him, you love him; and even though you do not see him now, you believe in him and are filled with an inexpressible and glorious joy, ^{9} for you are receiving the end result of your faith, the salvation of your souls.

So God sent His son, Jesus Christ, into the world to save us from our sins. How does this work?

What it means to be saved

First, let's consider the following passage from Hebrews Chapter 9.

> ^{27} **Just as people are destined to die once, and after that to face judgment, ^{28} so Christ was sacrificed once to take away the sins of many; and he will appear a second time, not to bear sin, but to bring salvation to those who are waiting for him.**

Now, imagine that after I die, I am in the courtroom before the judge to face that judgment. The judge looks at all my sins and says to me, "You are guilty of all these sins and your punishment is a big fine and a number of years in jail." But, I am dead. I have no money or possessions at this point and I have no more "living" time to serve in jail. So, I am destined for Hell . . . I cannot pay the penalty for my sins.

But God (the judge) looks across the room and sees His son, Jesus. Jesus speaks up and says that I believed in Him and I trusted Him with my life. He points out the evidence in my life of trusting and following Him. He says that He has paid the debt for all my sins. You see, God does not just forgive the debt I owe. My debt is paid in full by Jesus.

Remember, God is completely just. So every sin must be punished . . . paid for either by Jesus or by the sinner in Hell. Based on Jesus' testimony, I am declared righteous . . . not guilty of any sin! Because Jesus lived the perfect life, He is completely righteous. And, **"God made Him who had no sin to be sin for us, so that in Him we might become the righteousness of God"** (2 Corinthians 5:21). This is the great exchange . . . His righteousness for our sins!

Jesus was crucified on a cross. God, in His infinite mercy, put Him there and laid on Jesus all the punishments for our sins. Jesus took our sins and His death paid the debt we owed for all those sins. So, God has declared us as completely without sin because of the death of His Son. God raised Jesus from the dead and He sits at the right hand of God in Heaven and is our advocate.

All of this is a gift from God. Let's see what Jesus says about how we receive the Gospel in Mark Chapter 1.

> [14] **After John was put in prison, Jesus went into Galilee, proclaiming the good news of God.** [15] **"The time has come," he said. "The kingdom of God has come near. Repent and believe the good news!"**

So, when Jesus began His ministry, He indicated two conditions to enter the Kingdom of God:

- Repent and
- Believe in the Gospel.

J. C. Ryle's masterful and moving essay entitled *Repentance* urges us to repent. The primary passage for this call is Luke 13:3, "But unless you repent, you too will all perish."

In this essay, he describes three major components of repentance:

1. The nature of repentance
2. The necessity for repentance
3. The encouragement to repent.

His primary verse (Luke 13:3) is certainly a frightening warning to us all. But he concludes his essay with three sets of positive verses which should move us to action. They are listed below.

1. About Jesus Christ

    Hebrews 7:25   Acts 5:31

    Luke 19:10   Mark 2:17

    Matthew 11:28   John 6:37

    John 1:12   John 15:5

2. About God's promises

    Proverbs 28:13   1 John 1:9

    Matthew 5:3-6   Psalm 112

3. About God's nature

    Ezekiel 18:27   Psalm 51:1

    2 Peter 3:9   Ezekiel 33:11

    Luke 15:10   Jeremiah 17:10

But Ryle also provides a critical concluding thought. True repentance does not exist without faith (belief). The two are inseparable as we have just seen from Mark 1:15. Believing in the Gospel is another way of defining faith.

Let's take a closer look at what it means to believe . . . that is to have faith in the Gospel of Jesus Christ. Gospel means "good news." The "good news" is that God, through Jesus, has made a way for us to become a part of the Kingdom of God.

Oswald J. Smith (*What Does It mean To Believe?*) indicates that there are three steps in believing.

1. I must first **hear** the Gospel in order to believe
2. I must then **consent in my mind (and heart)** to what I hear . . . the Gospel
3. I must put my **trust** in Jesus
   (*I added <u>and heart</u> to # 2 above.*)

When I put my trust in Jesus, then He becomes both Savior and Lord for me. This means that I trust Him solely (Savior) . . . not my own works/deeds . . . for my salvation. In addition, it means that I trust in Him to be in charge of my life. He becomes first priority (Lord) instead of worldly things. For more on faith and trust, please see the classic passage from the Bible on salvation . . . Romans Chapter 3:19-26.

CONCLUSION
If you started reading this as one who did not believe in Jesus or were skeptical about Him and now have changed your position, then please consider this. Are you like the people in Acts, Chapter 2: 36-41, who after hearing Peter's sermon, were "cut to the heart" by the sin they committed? Do you have real "godly" sorrow for your sins?

A passage from 2 Corinthians, Chapter 7 will help us with that second question . . . especially verses 10 and 11.

> [8] Even if I caused you sorrow by my letter, I do not regret it. Though I did regret it—I see that my letter hurt you, but only for a little while—[9]yet now I am happy, not because you were made sorry, but because your sorrow led you to repentance. For you became sorrowful as God intended and so were not harmed in any way by us. **[10] Godly sorrow brings repentance that leads to salvation and leaves no regret, but worldly sorrow brings death. [11] See what this godly sorrow has produced in you: what earnestness, what eagerness to clear yourselves, what indignation, what alarm, what longing, what concern, what readiness to see justice done.**

If you feel that kind of sorrow and you now believe in Jesus, then let's rejoice and give all the credit to God. He has caused this change in you.

How does this change take place? Let's look at a passage from 2 Corinthians Chapter 4 for an explanation.

> **[6] For God, who said, "Let light shine out of darkness," made his light shine in our hearts to give us the light of the knowledge of God's glory displayed in the face of Christ.**

God described how He would work in this process in a number of places in the Bible. One place is the book of Ezekiel. God spoke about how He would work in His people in Ezekiel Chapter 36.

> [24]"For I will take you out of the nations; I will gather you from all the countries and bring you back into your own land. [25] I will sprinkle clean water on you, and you will be clean; I will cleanse you from all your impurities and from all

your idols. **²⁶ I will give you a new heart and put a new spirit in you; I will remove from you your heart of stone and give you a heart of flesh. ²⁷ And I will put my Spirit in you and move you to follow my decrees and be careful to keep my laws."**

Please note God's promise to give us a new heart and put a new spirit within us. He said something similar through the prophet Jeremiah in Chapter 31.

> ³³ "This is the covenant I will make with the people of Israel after that time," declares the LORD. **"I will put my law in their minds and write it on their hearts. I will be their God, and they will be my people. ³⁴ No longer will they teach their neighbor, or say to one another, 'Know the LORD,' because they will all know me, from the least of them to the greatest,"** declares the LORD. **"For I will forgive their wickedness and will remember their sins no more."**

This is another description of the "new covenant" God makes with His people. Notice His last promise. He will remember our sins no more!

Based on these promises it might be tempting to think that God does it all and we have no responsibility in this matter. Let's just sit back and let God take care of it. Wrong!! Read Romans Chapter 6 for our role in the new covenant.

God enables us to believe and act. But we have responsibility too! Remember what Jesus said. . . "Repent and believe." We must make the decisions necessary to change the fundamental course of our lives and to trust Jesus. God enables it but we must respond.

The basic point here is critical. God is sovereign and does work in our hearts and minds. That must come first. But, we must believe, trust, repent and follow Jesus. Jesus taught this in Luke 14 verses 25 through 34 when He explained the cost of being one of His disciples.

My prayer is that God has or will give you that new heart and spirit to enable you to become a child of His and we will see each other in Heaven. To God be the glory for the great things He has done and will do!

If you have experienced this kind of heartfelt, God-produced change in your life, then I recommend doing the following three things:

1. **Thank God** for working this miracle in your life and express your decision to trust Jesus and surrender your life to Him using the following prayer or something similar to it.

    Lord Jesus, I recognize that I am a sinner who falls short of your perfect standard. I trust in your death and resurrection as the only way I can live with you now and forever. I surrender my life to you to be used for your Kingdom and for the glory of God. Thank you Jesus for paying the debt I owe for my sins.

2. **Find a Christian friend** with whom you are comfortable and tell them about this change.
    If you find this to be uncomfortable, you might begin the conversation with the following question: How did

you become a Christian? Then describe what has taken place in your life.

3. **Find a Bible believing and Bible teaching church** and get involved with other Christians.
We are made for community. We need to be in a community of faith. We will not be successful as solo Christians. We need to experience the care, support, and teachings of a Christian community.

If this discussion leaves you unchanged or still questioning your beliefs, then I hope and pray that you will continue to seek answers to our "big" question and use the Bible to help you find those answers.

What Happens When I Die is a Life-Changing Issue!

If you have any questions about this discussion, please feel free to contact me at carterh1944@gmail.com.

A Mighty Fortress Is Our God

(Final stanza)

That word above all earthly powers,
no thanks to them, abideth;
the Spirit and the gifts are ours,
thru him who with us sideth.
Let goods and kindred go,
this mortal life also;
the body they may kill;
God's truth abideth still;
his kingdom is forever.

(Lyrics by Martin Luther)

Death . . . What's Next?

Book Resources

The Bible (NIV is quoted from in the document)

Arthur, Kay *Lord, Only You Can Change Me*, Colorado Springs, CO: WaterBrook Press, 2000

Assayas, Michka, *Bono in conversation with Michka Assayas,* New York, NY: Riverhead Books, 2005

Boice, James Montgomery, *Christ's Call to Discipleship,* Grand Rapids MI: Kregel Publishers, 2013

Boice, James Montgomery, *John, Volumes 1 – 5*, Grand Rapids MI: Baker Books, 2005

Boice, James Montgomery, *Living by the Book,* Grand Rapids MI: Baker Books, 2000

Boice, James Montgomery, *Renewing Your Mind in a Mindless World,* Grand Rapids MI: Kregel Publishers, 1993

Boice, James Montgomery, *Romans, Volumes 1 – 4,* Grand Rapids MI: Baker Books, 1995

Boice, James Montgomery, *The Parables of Jesus*, Chicago IL: Moody Publishers, 1983

Boice, James Montgomery, *To the Glory of God,* Grand Rapids MI: Baker Books, 2010

Boice, James Montgomery, *Whatever Happened to the Gospel of Grace,* Wheaton IL: Crossway, 2001

Bridges, Jerry, *The Pursuit of Holiness,* Colorado Springs, CO: NavPress, 2006

Bridges, Jerry, *Transforming Grace,* Colorado Springs, CO: NavPress, 2008

Calvin, John, *Institutes of the Christian Religion,* Carlisle, PA: The Banner of Truth, 2014

Calvin, John, *Calvin's Commentaries,* Grand Rapids MI: Baker Books, 2009 (23 volume set)

Carson, D.A., *The Difficult Doctrine of the Love of God,* Wheaton IL: Crossway, 2000

Chalmers, Thomas, *The Explusive Power of a New Affection,* New York: Robert Carter, 1848

Chanty, Walter J., *The Shadow of the Cross,* Carlisle, PA: The Banner of Truth, 1981

Chanty, Walter J., *Today's Gospel*, Carlisle, PA: The Banner of Truth, 1970

DeYoung, Kevin, *Just Do Something,* Chicago IL: Moody Publishers, 2009

Edwards, Jonathan, *Pursuing Holiness in the Lord,* Phillipsburg, NJ: The Jonathan Edwards Institute, 2005

Edwards, Jonathan, *Religious Affections,* Vancouver, British Columbia: Regent College Publishing, 1984

Edwards, Jonathan, *Sermons of Jonathan Edwards*, Peabody, MA: Hendrickson Publishers, Inc., 2005

Edwards, Jonathan, *Sinners in the hands of an Angry God,* Boston, MA: Kneeland and Green, 1741

Fraser, James, *A Treatise on Sanctification,* Audubon, NJ: Old Paths Publications, 1774

Greear, J. D., *Stop Asking Jesus Into Your Heart,* Nashville, TN: B&H Publishing Group, 2013

Grudem, Wayne, *Systematic Theology,* Grand Rapids MI: Zondervan, 1994

Hendricks, Howard G. and William D., *Living by the Book,* Chicago IL: Moody Publishers, 2007

Hybels, Bill, *Courageous Leadership,* Grand Rapids MI: Zondervan, 2009

Keller, Timothy, *Counterfeit Gods,* New York, NY: Penguin Group, 2009

Keller, Timothy, *Judges for You,* USA: thegoodbook Co, 2013

Keller, Timothy, *Prodigal God,* New York, NY: Penguin Group, 2008

Kendall, R. T., *The Sermon on the Mount,* Minneapolis MN: Baker, 2011

Lewis, C. S., *Mere Christianity,* San Francisco CA: HarperCollins, 2001

Lloyd-Jones, D. Martyn, *2 Peter,* Carlisle, PA: The Banner of Truth, 1983

Lloyd-Jones, D. Martyn, *Joy Unspeakable,* OK: David C. Cook,1994

Lloyd-Jones, D. Martyn, *Spiritual Depression*, Grand Rapids, MI: William B. Eerdmans Publishing Co., 1965

Lloyd-Jones, D. Martyn, *Studies in the Sermon on the Mount*, Grand Rapids, MI: William B. Eerdmans Publishing Co., 1976

Lloyd-Jones, D. Martyn, *The Cross,* Wheaton IL: Crossway, 1986

MacArthur, John, *1 – 3 John*, Chicago IL: Moody Publishers, 2007

MacArthur, John, *The Gospel According to the Apostles,* Nashville, TN: Thomas Nelson,2000

MacArthur, John, *The Gospel According to the Jesus,* Grand Rapids MI: Zondervan, 2008

MacArthur, John, *The Jesus Answer Book,* Nashville, TN: Thomas Nelson, 2014

MacArthur, John, *The Truth About Grace,* Nashville, TN: Thomas Nelson, 2012

MacArthur, John, *Twelve Ordinary Men*, Nashville, TN: Thomas Nelson, 2002

MaHaney, C. J., *Humility: True Greatness,* Colorado Springs, CO: Multnomah Books, 2005

Manz, Charles C., *The Leadership Wisdom of Jesus,* San Francisco, CA: Berrett-Kohler, 2008

Miller, C. John, *Repentance: A Daring Call to Surrender,* Fort Washington, PA: CLC Publishers, 2009

Morgan, Robert J., *Then Sings My Soul,* Nashville, TN: Thomas Nelson, 2003

Morris, Leon, *Jesus is the Christ,* Grand Rapids, MI: William B. Eerdmans Publishing Company, 1989

Morris, Leon, *The Gospel According to John,* Grand Rapids, MI: William B. Eerdmans Publishing Company, 1995

Morris, Leon, *Revelation,* Grand Rapids, MI: William B. Eerdmans Publishing Company, 1987

North, Brownlow, *The Prodigal Son*, London: Silver Trumpet Publishers, Ltd., 1989

North, Brownlow, *The Rich Man and Lazarus*, London: The Banner of Truth, 1968

Owen, John, *The Mortification of Sin,* USA: Create Space, 2013

Tozer, A. W., *The Pursuit of God*, Ventura, CA: Regal, 2013

Tripp, Paul David, *Forever,* Grand Rapids MI: Zondervan, 2011

Spurgeon, Charles Haddon, *All of Grace,* Shippensburg, PA: Destiny Image, 2007

Spurgeon, Charles Haddon, *Morning & Evening,* New Kensington, PA: Whitaker House, 2001.

Stedman, Ray C., *Authentic Christianity*, Grand Rapids, MI: Discovery House, 1996

Stott, John R. W., *Confess Your Sins*, Waco, TX: Word Books, 1974

Stott, John R. W., *The Message of the Sermon on the Mount*, Downers Grove, IL: Inter Varsity Press1978

Piper, John, *A Peculiar Glory,* Wheaton, IL: Inter Varsity Press, 2016

Piper, John*, Don't Waste your Life,* Wheaton IL: Crossway, 2009

Piper, John, *Future Grace*, Colorado Springs, CO: Multnomah Books, 1995

Piper, John, *God is the Gospel,* Wheaton IL: Crossway, 2005

Piper, John, *Life as a Vapor,* Colorado Springs, CO: Multnomah Books, 2004

Piper, John, *The Passion of Jesus Christ,* Wheaton IL: Crossway, 2004

Platt, David, *Radical,* Colorado Springs, CO: Multnomah Books, 2010

Willard, Dallas, *Renewing the Christian Mind,* New York, NY: HarperCollins Publishers, 2016

Web Resources

www.desiringgod.com – Devotionals, sermons and articles by John Piper

www.spurgeon.org/resource-library/sermons/recently-added – The sermons of Charles H. Spurgeon

www.biblegateway.com/devotionals/morning-and-evening/today – Morning and Evening daily devotionals by Charles H. Spurgeon

Acknowledgements

I am writing this primarily for my family and friends... all of whom I love very much. My greatest desire for each of them is that they are saved by the grace of God, through faith alone, by the work of Christ alone, to the glory of God alone, as recorded in the Bible alone. And, therefore, they can face death with the calm assurance of that saving faith.

However, this work may be of help to folks I don't even know. I hope and pray that it will be.

One thing I do know. This work will not change a single heart . . . God does that. But He does use the works of His creation to assist in that process.

I want to acknowledge those who have meant so much to me in this journey of faith and reflection. So, my heartfelt thanks go out to all of those listed here.

> The current and former pastors of First United Methodist Church Statesboro Georgia
> The current and former pastors, elders and deacons of East Cooper Baptist Church Charleston SC
> The pastors and deacons of First Baptist Church of Charleston SC
> All those other saints whose teachings and writings have shaped my understanding about God

I mention a few specifically by name because of their unique influence:

> Don Adams
> Carter Berkley
> Marshall Blalock

Andy Boyer
Buster Brown
Dave Bruner
Elick and Margaret Bullington
Kenny Caldwell
Hugh Davis
Dave Golden
John Graham
John Grinalds
Bill Hatcher
Dean Henderson
Dan Legare
Steve Lindenmeyer
Patricia McArver (*editorial advisor*)
Robert McCants
Frank and Lisa Morris
Rick Mosteller
Gilbert Ramsey
Josh Romine (*reviewer*)
J. Robert Smith
Claude Tackett
Carrie and Ed Timmerman

Finally, the support and love of family members has been enabling and inspirational.

Bill & Carol Carter	Parents
Brenda	Wife
Ashley	Daughter
Bill & Erica	Son and Daughter-in-law
Lauren, Lindsey & Courtney	Grandchildren
Grandparents, aunt and uncle, cousins and in-laws	

Other works by Harry Carter

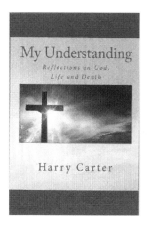

My Understanding is a study of Biblical principles reflected in the Old and New Testaments. The author shares his exploration of what the Bible says about God and Jesus Christ and offers ten conclusions he believes reflect the basic message of God's love and our salvation. His concluding chapter *How then should I live?* reveals the answers he has developed during his spiritual journey. Any Christian seeking a closer relationship with God will find this work a thought-provoking study.

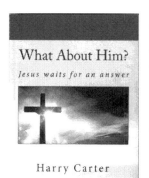

Christians and many non-Christians acknowledge Jesus or profess some level of belief in Him. But what does that mean? In his second book on biblical teachings, Harry Carter asks readers to reflect deeply on a question that is fundamental to faith and salvation.

What About Him? presents a simple question that challenges the reader to explore the very foundation of our Christian faith. Carter takes a systematic approach to analyzing what the Bible – the one true word of God – says about Jesus. *What About Him*? is a thought-provoking work that will assist readers in confronting their own beliefs about Jesus, the Christian faith and the path to salvation.

Made in the USA
Middletown, DE
19 March 2024